P.E.T.

PIERRE ELLIOTT TRUDEAU

and his unearthly adventures

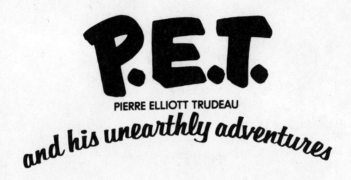

P.E.T.
PIERRE ELLIOTT TRUDEAU
and his unearthly adventures

an illustrated history of Trudeaumania

by Jude Waples

AVON BOOKS OF CANADA
PUBLISHERS OF BARD, CAMELOT, DISCUS AND FLARE BOOKS

P.E.T. PIERRE ELLIOTT TRUDEAU AND HIS UNEARTHLY
ADVENTURES is an original publication of Avon Books. This
work has never before appeared in book form.

AVON BOOKS
A division of
The Hearst Corporation
959 Eighth Avenue
New York, New York 10019

First Avon Printing, June, 1983

AVON TRADEMARK REG. U.S. PAT. OFF. AND IN
OTHER COUNTRIES, MARCA REGISTRADA, HECHO EN
U.S.A.

Printed in the U.S.A.

DON 10 9 8 7 6 5 4 3 2 1

P.E.T.

PIERRE ELLIOTT TRUDEAU

and his unearthly adventures

In the following pages the author has relied heavily on P.E.T.'s own words to tell the tale. All quotations appear in italics.

Once it was believed that gods
walked upon the earth...

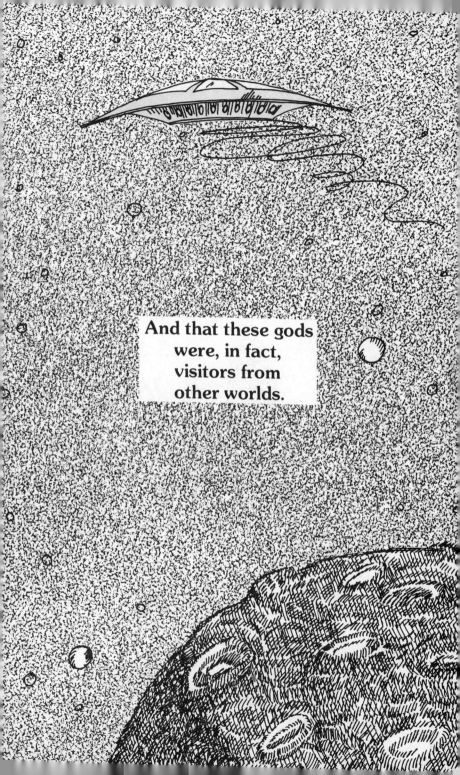

And that these gods were, in fact, visitors from other worlds.

and heroes.

Many believe that our planet is still inhabite

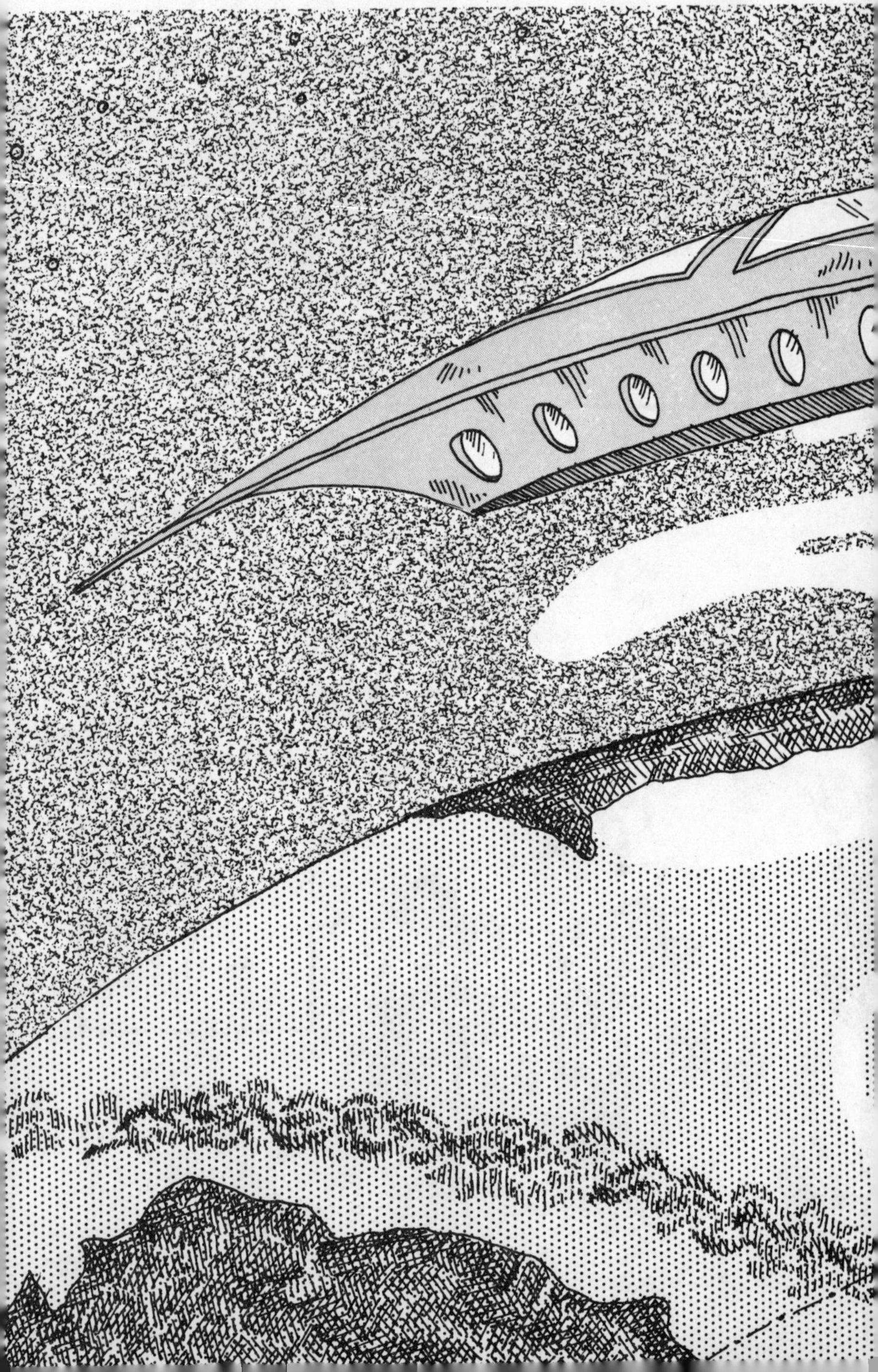

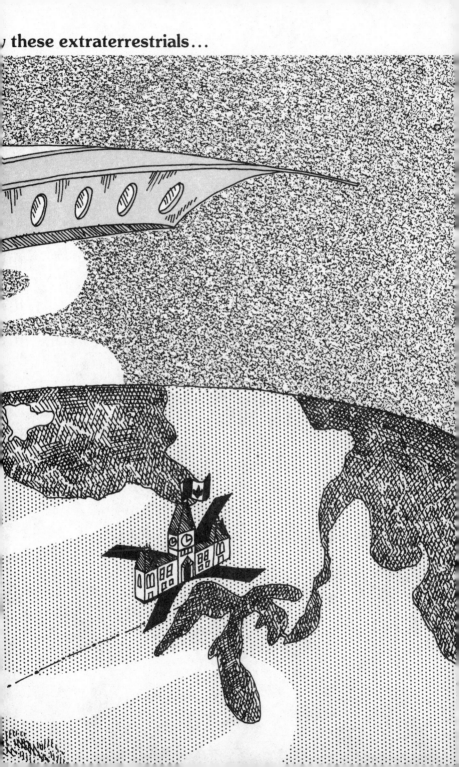

And that they are with us today.

But we know this isn't true...

or is it?

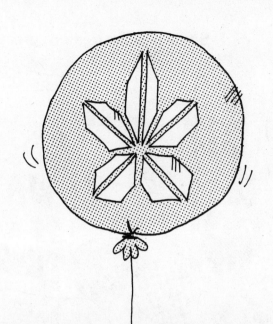

"TRUDEAUMANIA"

*Let us not lose ourselves
in a fog of negativism.*

Signs read: PUSH P.E.T. · P.E.T. · PIERRE · WAY TO GO TRUDEAU · PIERRE AND CANADA OUR FUTURE · LUCKY PIERRE

With P.E.T.'s superior intellect and devotion to liberalism it was only natural that he take over the reins of power.

Well... most of them.

Recognizing that desperate times
require desperate measures,
P.E.T. created the Supergroup,
a new group with new ideas.
Not better…just new.

As demigods their purpose
was to create bureaucracy:
to study the issues troubling
the nation; to evaluate,
coordinate, rectify and
speculate; to itemize,
systematize, execute and
prioritize; to reform, inform,
regulate and transform.

Together they strived for
consensus...and reached no
conclusions at all!

You can't solve
this problem by
just throwing
money at it.

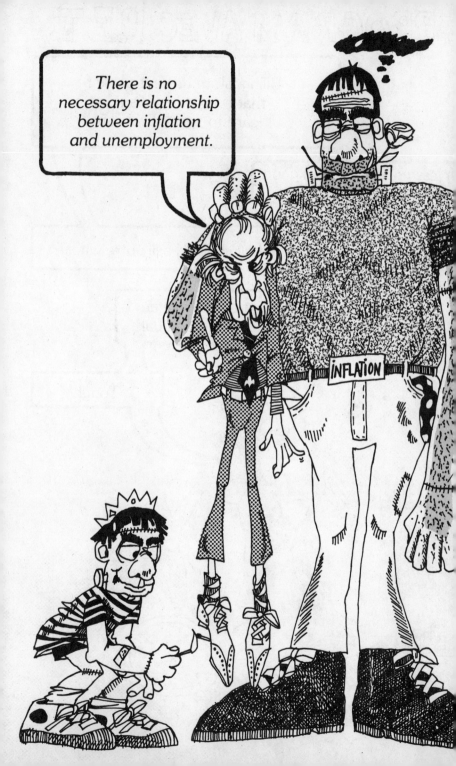

P.E.T. and his Supergroup
devoted themselves to the cause
of bilingualism and failed to
create jobs. Instead of uniting
the country P.E.T. found himself
surrounded by people who were
now demanding jobs in two
languages. He appealed to
Canadians, saying
*What is this hostility out
there that assumes that
whatever the government
does is wrong?*

And then he declared
*We have brought down
the worst plague we
have had—inflation.*

During the halcyon days of
power when P.E.T. was getting
a hell of a lot of fun
out of being Prime Minister,
there were those who sought
to undermine his ideals
and separate themselves
from his political grasp.
Together they spread
discontent, telling Canadians
that the road to hell is
paved with rational ideas.

And he went to his head.

Philosopher King? Well after all
most people *don't want to be governed
by people less good than themselves*
so P.E.T. walked across the water of his
$200,000 pool and accepted the crown.

Unfortunately his egotism grew proportionately with his ar

nce, proving that power corrupts even a supreme being!

And soon P.E.T. believed it
was nobler to let others suffer the
slings and arrows of
outrageous fortune.

**The people began to notice
and grumbled amongst themselves...
can mere man become a god?**

P.E.T. himself began to think that not all was right in his kingdom.

It certainly wasn't the government's intention to create unemployme

Welcome

If they don't like it here,

let them find another country.

Get off your ass—

get out there and work.

to the 80's

Whether or not it is clear to you,
no doubt
the universe is unfolding as it should.

Frankly my dear...I don't give a damn!

But when P.E.T. asked us to tighten our belts,
we asked him to retire.

P.E.T. just shrugged and pointed out
that after all *No government can promise*
everything to everybody,
everywhere, all the time.
Sometimes
it has to
say
NO.

PAGE 15. "If you want to show up as an original thinker, you don't have to rely on turtlenecks or on sandals." Trudeau's answer to a question about his change to a more conservative style of dress.
Globe & Mail, April 15, 1978.

PAGE 16. "I've always said I think an individual should put his destiny before the institution." A comment made in 1972.
Globe & Mail, November 22, 1979.

PAGE 18. "I get a certain amount of pleasure from daring people to do things in a certain way. That's why I'm enjoying this period of my political life." Part of Trudeau's answer to a question on the economy.
Toronto Star, July 10, 1982

PAGE 19. "Mangez de la merde!" Trudeau's response to the group of Montreal mail truck drivers who were angry over the government takeover of Montreal postal operations.
Toronto Star, February 2, 1971.

PAGE 20. "Fuddle Duddle." The Prime Minister claims to have said fuddle duddle, not f--- off, during a debate on the economy in the House of Commons.
Toronto Star, February 17, 1971.

PAGE 21. The words of P.E.T. as Queen Victoria were inspired by a statement Trudeau made regarding Parliament. "It's a place where men are shouting...and I find that vulgar, it offends me."
Northern Magus by Richard Gwyn (Toronto:McClelland and Stewart, 1980), page 58.

PAGE 22. "Why are Canadians so much like mushrooms? Because their government keeps them in the dark and feeds them horse manure."
From a list of famous Trudeauisms.
Toronto Star, April 15, 1978.

PAGE 31. "Let us not lose ourselves in a fog of negativism."
From a list of famous Trudeauisms.
Toronto Star, April 15, 1978.

PAGE 33.   "I was pushed."
How Trudeau described his decision to run for leadership of the federal Liberal party.
Northern Magus, page 66.

PAGE 36.   "He's a totally unprincipled man..."
A statement by Malcolm Muggeridge in an interview with *Weekend Magazine*.
Globe & Mail Weekend Magazine, Volume 24, #12. 23 March, 1974.

PAGE 37.   "It's not a perfect job, but it sure beats working."
Trudeau's answer when questioned about how he liked the job of Prime Minister.
Toronto Star, October 8, 1975.

PAGE 38.   "my best feature is my bum."
A statement made by Margaret Trudeau published in *People* magazine.
Northern Magus, page 214

PAGE 40.   "new group with new ideas."
From an interview with Patrick Watson, who used the phrase in a question. Trudeau jumped on it and used it to characterise his new, "fresh" approach.
Northern Magus, page 68.

PAGE 40.   "Zap, you're frozen."
One of the phrases Trudeau used to ridicule Stanfield's proposed wage and price controls.
Northern Magus, page 158.

PAGE 43.   "You can't solve this problem by just throwing money at it."
Trudeau's thoughts on the poor economy.
Toronto Star, March 27, 1982.

PAGE 46.   "There is no necessary relationship between inflation and unemployment."
Globe & Mail, November 22, 1979.

PAGE 47.   "What is this hostility out there that assumes that whatever the government does is wrong?"
Globe & Mail, November 18, 1978.

PAGE 47.   "We have brought down the worst plague we have had—inflation."
Toronto Star, September 21, 1976.

PAGE 48.   "Just watch me."
Trudeau's response when CBC correspondent Tim Ralfe asked him how far he would go in using force during the F.L.Q. crisis.
Northern Magus, page 119.

PAGE 49. "Well there are a lot of bleeding hearts…"
Trudeau's response to the claim that he went overboard in the use of force during the F.L.Q. crisis.
Northern Magus, page 120.

PAGE 50. "A hell of a lot of fun."
Trudeau's comment on how he was enjoying being Prime Minister.
Toronto Star, August 12, 1969.

PAGE 55. "We can't build a future with someone who has already packed his bags to leave."
Trudeau's statement about working with the Parti Quebecois.
Toronto Star, December 1, 1980.

PAGE 59. "asshole"
President Nixon's assessment of Trudeau, taped in Nixon's office on March 22, 1973.
Globe & Mail, October 26, 1974.

PAGE 59. "I think he has a natural born talent for getting slapped in the face."
Levesque's comment after being insulted by Trudeau in the offices of the *Cité Libre*.
Northern Magus, page 236.

PAGES 60-61. "Don't want to be governed by people less good than themselves."
Trudeau on why he is still leader of the Liberal party.
Toronto Star, December 15, 1978.

PAGE 65. "We're in the process of survival."
Lalonde used these words to describe the current economic hard times while treating ten journalists to a lunch of cold pizza and beer.
Macleans, Vol. 95, #45, 8 November, 1982.

PAGE 66. "I just can't stand those guys."
Trudeau's opinion of most reporters.
Northern Magus, page 319.

PAGE 66. "The media and the opposition are the twin enemies of the Liberal government and it's time to fight back."
Toronto Star, November 18, 1978.

PAGE 70. "If I can be permitted to turn around a phrase I would say that I am kind of sorry I won't have you to kick around anymore."
Trudeau used this famous Nixon quote in his speech when he resigned from the leadership of the Liberal party.
Toronto Star, November 21, 1979.

PAGE 72. "It certainly wasn't the government's intention to create unemployment."
From a list of famous Trudeauisms.
Toronto Star Today Magazine, 17 April, 1982.

PAGE 76. "an old softie."
Trudeau said "You've always known I'm an old softie" to explain his tears as he announced his resignation as leader of the Liberal party.
Northern Magus, page 340.

PAGE 77. "Considering the alternative, I think I am the best man."
Trudeau's answer to questions about his possible retirement.
Toronto Star, November 15, 1978.

PAGES 78-79. "Welcome to the 80's."
Opening words of Trudeau's victory speech.
Toronto Star, February 19, 1980.

PAGES 78-79. *"Whether or not it is clear to you, no doubt the universe is unfolding as it should."*
Trudeau quoted from Desiderata after almost losing 1972 election.
Northern Magus, page 137.

PAGES 78-79. "If they don't like it here, let them find another country."
Toronto Star, April 15, 1978.

PAGES 78-79. "Get off your ass—get out there and work."
To a group protesting high unemployment in British Columbia.
Toronto Star, April 8, 1979.

PAGE 80. "Canada is a country whose main exports are hockey players and cold fronts. Our main imports are baseball players and acid rain."
Comments made at the 1980 All-Star baseball game.
Toronto Star, July 14, 1982.

PAGE 81. "For all its sham, drudgery and broken dreams, the world is still a beautiful place."
Trudeau quoted from *Desiderata* again when he resigned as leader of the federal Liberal party.
Globe & Mail, November 22, 1979.

PAGE 84. "I must say in all frankness that a difficult winter lies ahead...I believe, however, that it can also be a decisive winter for our economy and for our country."
From the first episode of the Pierre Elliot Trudeau miniseries on the CBC.

PAGE 86. "Life in politics is always exciting."
Trudeau is told that Nixon called him an asshole. Trudeau says he has been called "worse things by worse men" and then that "life in politics is always exciting."
Globe & Mail, October 26, 1974.

PAGE 86. "No government can promise everything to everybody, everywhere, all the time. Sometimes it has to say no."
Toronto Star, February 6, 1980.